The Private Journal of a Journey From Boston to New York in the Year 1704

THE

PRIVATE JOURNAL

OF A

Journey from Boston to New York,

IN

THE YEAR 1704.

KEPT BY

MADAM KNIGHT.

ALBANY:
FRANK H. LITTLE.
1865.

PREFACE.

IN the month of October, 1704, Madam Sarah Knight traveled on horseback from Boston to New Haven. She continued her journey to New York in the following December, and after staying there two weeks returned to New Haven, and thence in March to Boston. During this time she kept a journal, which was for many years preserved among her descendants, but now is believed to be lost. This journal was published in New York in 1825, and in the introduction to that edition it is stated that "the original orthography has been carefully preserved." The present edition is an exact reprint of the former, including the introduction, with the addition of a few notes.

Madam Sarah Knight was born April 19, 1666. She was the daughter of Capt. Thomas

Kemble, a merchant of Boston, and of Elizabeth Trarice, his wife.[1]   He was a native of Great Britain, and resided in Charlestown as early as 1651, and for several years afterwards.[2]   For many years he was an attorney or agent of Mr. Robert Rich, a merchant of London.[3]   He had several children, one of whom, John, a cooper or carpenter, died in New York, and by a will made in 1695, gave his lands and houses to his wife for her life, then to Madam Knight for her life, and then to her daughter.[1]

Before the birth of Sarah, Capt. Kemble had moved to Boston; and there in 1676 he built a large house on the easterly side of Moon street, corner of Moon street court, about half way from Sun Court street to Fleet street. The house was demolished in 1832, or soon after, and a tobacco warehouse erected, which has now been con-

[1] Savage's *Genealogical Dictionary*, III, 21, *et seq.*

[2] Littell's *Living Age*, LVII, 964, a very full and interesting article, by Mr. William R Deane, who has gathered nearly all the facts that are known about Madam Knight, and has kindly permitted their use   Much of this preface is taken from that article, which is referred to, for convenience, by his initials

[3] W. R. D.

verted into the Catholic church.[1] He lived in this house until his death, January 29, 1688-9. His wife survived him until December 19, 1712. The grave stones of both are in the Copp's Hill burying ground.[2]

Sarah Kemble was married to Richard Knight of Boston, "a Captain of a London trader."[3] He died abroad, but in what year is not ascertained. Mr. Deane says that his wife supposed him to be living in 1706, when she signed as his attorney;[4] but the notice in the *Historical Magazine*, just referred to, states that her journey in 1704 was to claim some of his property in New York.

The fact that he is not mentioned in the journal seems to favor the latter of these views. He had had a former wife, Remember Grafton, the daughter of Nathaniel Grafton, of Salem;[1] and he is said by one authority to have been "bred a carver."[5]

Soon after her return from the New York

[1] *Historical Magazine*, ix, 93, *et seq*

[2] W R D.

[3] *Historical Magazine*, ix, 93, *et seq.*

[4] W. R D , referring to Middlesex Reg. Deeds, iii, 463.

[5] Savage's *Genealogical Dictionary*

journey Madam Knight opened a school for children.   Dr. Franklin and Dr. Samuel Mather
were among her scholars.   As she was the only
surviving child of her parents she continued to
keep school in the house built by her father
until 1714.   She then sold the estate to Peter
Papillion; and it became afterwards the property
of Hannah, wife of Dr. Samuel Mather.   In the
year 1763 Dr. Mather had the house new glazed;
and one pane of glass was preserved as a curiosity till it was lost when Charlestown was burnt
in 1765.   That pane bore the following lines
written with a diamond:

> Through many toils and many frights
>   I have returned, poor Sarah Knights
> Over great rocks and many stones
>   God has preserved from fractured bones

It was as a schoolmistress that she acquired
the title of Madam; and she is said to have been
noted for teaching composition.[1]

Elizabeth, the only child of Madam Knight,

---

[1] *Historical Magazine,* as cited above   In his autobiography Dr.
Franklin does not mention Madam Knight; but he states that he
was sent to the grammar school at eight years of age; and this
would correspond with the time when Madam Knight gave up

was born in Boston, May 8th, 1689, and was married there by Dr. Increase Mather to Colonel John Livingston of New London, Oct. 1st, 1713.[1] She was his second wife. His first wife was met by Madam Knight and is mentioned in the journal. Mrs Elizabeth Livingston survived her husband; but had no children. A table of freestone with this inscription perpetuates her memory:

> "Interd vnder this stone is the body of Madam Elizabeth Livingston, relict of Col John Livingstone of New London, who departed this life March 17th A D 1735-6 in the 48th year of her age "[2]

It was undoubtedly the marriage of her daughter which induced Madam Knight to sell her house. About this time she removed to the neighborhood of Norwich and New London, Ct., and there spent the remainder of an energetic and active life.

[1] W R D.

[2] Miss Frances M Caulkins's *History of New London*, 365 Many of the subsequent details of Madam Knight's life, after she removed from Boston, are copied by permission from Miss Caulkins' History, and from a letter written by her to Mr. Deane in 1858, and printed in the article already mentioned.

In 1717 a silver cup for the communion service was presented by her to the church in Norwich; and the town by vote, August 12th, gave her liberty to "sit in the pew where she used to sit."[1] In 1718, March 26th, Madam Knight and six other persons were presented in one indictment "for selling strong drink to the Indians." They were fined twenty shillings and costs. It is added to the record, "Mrs. Knight accused her maid, Ann Clark, of the fact." After this period Madam Knight appears as a land purchaser in the North Parish of New London, generally as a partner with Joseph Bradford. Col. Livingston had purchased a great amount of land from the Mohegan Indians, which he had gradually parted with. Madam Knight and Mr. Bradford repurchased much of this land. One deed conveyed to them more than two thousand acres for which they paid £1000; and another deed was for about half that extent.

She was also a pew holder in the new church

[1] In those early days places were assigned, or, as the phrase was, "the meeting house was seated" by the authority of the town The "chief seats in the synagogues" were matters of great interest and ambition and sometimes of much controversy.

built in the North Parish of New London about
1724, and was sometimes styled of Norwich and
sometimes of New London. She retained her
dwelling house in Norwich; but her farms
where she spent a portion of her time, were
within the bounds of New London. On one
of these, the Livingston farm, upon the Norwich
road, she kept entertainment for travelers, and
is called innkeeper. At this place she died,
Sept. 25th, 1727, and was brought to New
London for interment. A gray headstone, of
which an exact impression is given on a following page, marks the place.[1] The only child
of Madam Knight, Elizabeth, relict of Col.
John Livingston, survived her, and presented
her inventory, which comprised two farms in
Mohegan with housing and mills, £1600, and
estate in Norwich, £210.

The journal which is here reprinted, had
been carefully preserved·in manuscript in the
Christophers family, to whom it came after
the death of Mr. Livingston; Sarah, wife of
Christopher Christophers, who was a Prout, of

[1] Miss Caulkins's *History of New London*, 372, *et seq.*

2

New Haven, and a relative, being appointed
to administer on her estate. From a descendant
of this Mrs. Christophers, viz: Mrs. Ichabod
Wetmore, of Middletown, the manuscript was
obtained for publication. It had been neatly
copied into a small book.[1] The original was
not returned to Mrs. Wetmore, and, with the
exception of a single leaf, has unfortunately been
destroyed.[2]

Madam Knight's business on this journey was,
as she says, the distribution of an estate and
one evidently in which she had a personal interest. It may possibly have been that of her
brother John, who had died in New York a
few years previously, or perhaps that of her
husband, as stated by Mrs. Hannah Mather
Crocker.[3] A suggestion has been made that it
was the estate of Caleb Trowbridge; but this is
not probable, as her name appears in 1704 as a

[1] Miss Caulkins's *History of New London*, 373.

[2] It appears from Mr. Deane's article that this leaf was then in
possession of Mr. Theodore Dwight of New York, who edited the
journal.

[3] *Historical Magazine*, IX, 93.

witness to the papers by which that estate was settled.[1]

It is evident from her journal that Madam Knight was energetic and observing; that she had some imagination and a good perception of the ludicrous. She seems also to have been free from that strict and narrow character which is generally attributed to the Puritan of early New England. She rides a few miles on Sunday, and considers the prohibition of "innocent merriment among young people," to be "rigid." She makes jokes on Mr. Devil's name, which, only a few years earlier, might have convicted her of witchcraft, if they had come to the ears of Cotton Mather. And although absent from home for five months, and a visitor with at least two or three clergymen, she gives no account of any sermon which she may have heard. Her silence in this particular may have been because there was more novelty in the matters which she narrates.

Wherever it is possible to make the test, her journal will be found accurate even in slight

[1] W. R D

matters.   It may therefore with good reason be
relied upon in all its details.   .

In the introduction to the former edition it is
said that over the same journey which Madam
Knight made, "we proceed at our ease without
exposure, and almost without fatigue, in a day
and a half."   A penciled note made in 1849 to
a copy of the edition adds: " now performed by
rail road in ten hours."   That time is now re-
duced to eight.   One may venture to think that
the speed of travel will never be carried to a
much higher degree than it has now reached.

Albany, 1865.

HERE LYETH THE BODY
OF Mrs SARAH KNIGHT
WHO DIED SEP^T THE 25th
1727 IN THE 62^D YEAR
OF   HER   AGE

THE

PRIVATE JOURNAL

KEPT BY

MADAM KNIGHT,

ON A JOURNEY

FROM BOSTON TO NEW YORK,

IN THE YEAR 1704

FROM THE ORIGINAL MANUSCRIPT.

INTRODUCTION.

THIS is not a work of fiction, as the scarcity of old American manuscripts may induce some to imagine; but it is a faithful copy from a diary in the author's own hand-writing, compiled soon after her return home, as it appears, from notes recorded daily while on the road. She was a resident of Boston, and a lady of uncommon literary attainments, as well as of great taste and strength of mind. She was called Madam Knight, out of respect to her character, according to a custom once common in New England; but what was her family name the publishers have not been able to discover.

The object proposed in printing this little work is not only to please those who have partially studied the progressive history of our country, but to direct the attention of others to subjects of that description, unfashionable as they still are; and also to remind the public that documents, even as unpretending as the following, may possess a real value, if they contain facts which will be hereafter sought for to illustrate interesting periods in our history.

It is to be regretted that the brevity of the work should have allowed the author so little room for the display of the cultivated mind and the brilliant fancy which frequently betray themselves in the course of the narrative; and no one can rise from the perusal without wishing some happy chance might yet discover more full delineations of life and character from the same practiced hand. Subjects so closely connected with ourselves ought to excite a degree of curiosity and interest, while we are generally so ready to open our minds and our libraries to the most minute details of foreign governments, and the modes and men of distant countries, with which we can have only a collateral connection.

In copying the following work for the press, the original orthography has been carefully preserved, in some cases, it may be, so far as to retain the errors of the pen, for fear of introducing any unwarrantable modernism. The punctuation was very hasty, and therefore has not been regarded. Two interruptions occur in the original near the commencement, which could not be supplied; and in a few instances it has been thought proper to make short omissions, but none of them materially affect the narrative.

The reader will find frequent occasion to compare the state of things in the time of our author with that of the present period, particularly with regard to the number of the inhabitants, and the facilities and accommodations prepared for travelers. Over that tract of country where she traveled about a fortnight on horseback, under the direction of a hired guide, with frequent risks of life and limb, and sometimes without food or shelter for many miles, we proceed at our ease, without exposure and almost without fatigue, in a day and a half,

through a well peopled land, supplied with good
stage coaches and public houses, or the still
greater luxuries of the elegant steam boats which
daily traverse our waters.

THE

JOURNAL

OF

MADAM KNIGHT.

Monday, Octb'r. y⁰ second, 1704.—About three o'clock afternoon, I begun my Journey from Boston to New Haven; being about two Hundred Mile. My Kinsman, Capt. Robert Luist,[1] waited on me as farr as Dedham, where I was to meet y⁰ Western post.[2]

[1] Robert Luist, shopkeeper of Charlestown, with others, signed a receipt for his share of Mrs. Livingston's estate. Miss Caulkins's letter, W. R. D. In Savage's *Genealogical Dictionary* this name is found under LEWIS

[2] Letters patent, granting to Thomas Neale for twenty-one years the franchise of establishing a Post Office, were issued in 1691, and in 1693 the General Court of Massachusetts, under the authority of those letters, established a "General Letter Office"

The western post was the post between Boston and New York. A few years later, during the "winter months," it set out once a

I vissitted the Reverd. Mr. Belcher,[1] ye Minister of ye town, and tarried there till evening, in hopes ye post would come along. But he not coming, I resolved to go to Billingses where he used to lodg, being 12 miles further. But being ignorant of the way, Mad^m Billings,[2] seing no persuasions of her good spouses or hers could prevail with me to Lodg there that night, Very kindly went wyth me to ye Tavern, where I hoped to get my guide, And desired the Hostess to inquire of her guests whether any of them would go with mee. But they being tyed by the Lipps to a pewter engine, scarcely allowed themselves time to say what clownish

[*Here half a page of the MS. is gone.*]

Peices of eight, I told her no, I would not be accessary to such extortion.

Then John shan't go, sais shee. No, indeed, shan't hee; And held forth at that rate a long

fortnight, going alternately to Saybrook and to Hartford, and at those places exchanging mails with the New York rider.

Mass Hist. Col 3d Series, XII, 48

[1] The Rev. Joseph Belcher, who was graduated at Harvard in 1690 and ordained at Dedham Nov. 29, 1693.

[2] Probably a misprint for "Madam Belcher."

time, that I began to fear I was got among the Quaking tribe, beleeving not a Limbertong'd sister among them could outdo Madm. Hostes.

Upon this, to my no small surprise, son John arrose, and gravely demanded what I would give him to go with me? Give you, sais I, are you John? Yes, says he, for want of a Better, And behold! this John look't as old as my Host, and perhaps had bin a man in the last Century. Well, Mr. John, sais I, make your demands. Why, half a pss. of eight and a dram, sais John. I agreed, and gave him a Dram (now) in hand to bind the bargain.

My hostess catechis'd John for going so cheep, saying his poor wife would break her heart

[*Here another half page of the MS. is gone.*]

His shade on his Hors resembled a Globe on a Gate post. His habitt, Hors and furniture, its looks and goings Incomparably answered the rest.

Thus Jogging on with an easy pace, my Guide telling mee it was dangero's to Ride hard in the Night, (wh^ch his horse had the sence to avoid,) Hee entertained me with the Adventurs he had passed by late Rideing, and eminent Dangers he had escaped, so that, Remembring the Hero's in Parismus[1] and the Knight of the Oracle, I didn't know but I had mett wth a Prince disguis'd.

When we had Ridd about an how'r, wee come into a thick swamp, wch. by, Reason of a great fogg, very much startled mee, it being now very Dark.   But nothing dismay'd John : Hee had encountered a thousand and a thousand such Swamps, having a Universall Knowledge in the woods; and readily Answered all my inquiries wch. were not a few.

In about an how'r, or something more, after we left the Swamp, we come to Billinges, where I was to Lodg.   My Guide dismounted and very Complasantly help't me down and shewd the door, signing to me wth his hand to Go in; wch I Gladly did—But had not gone many steps into

---

[1] Parismus, the renowned prince of Bohemia, his most famous, delectable and pleasant history; containing his noble battails brought against the Persians, his love to Laurana, the King's daughter of Thessaly, and his strange adventures in the desolate Island &c. London, T. Creede, 1598 Eighteen editions of it are recorded during the next hundred years Written by Edward Ford.

the Room, ere I was Interogated by a young
Lady I understood afterwards was the Eldest
daughter of the family, with these, or words to
this purpose, (viz.) Law for mee—what in the
world brings You here at this time a night?—I
never see a woman on the Rode so Dreadfull late,
in all the days of my versall life. Who are
You? Where are You going? I'me scar'd out
of my witts—with much now of the same Kind.
I stood aghast, Prepareing to reply, when in
comes my Guide—to him Madam turn'd, Roreing
out: Lawfull heart, John, is it You?—how de
do! Where in the world are you going with
this woman? Who is she? John made no
Ansr. but sat down in the corner, fumbled out
his black Junk, and saluted that instead of Debb;
she then turned agen to mee and fell anew into
her silly questions, without asking me to sitt
down.

I told her she treated me very Rudely, and I
did not think it my duty to answer her unman-
nerly Questions. But to get ridd of them, I told
her I come there to have the post's company
with me to-morrow on my Journey, &c. Miss

star'd awhile, drew a chair, bid me sitt, And then run up stairs and putts on two or three Rings, (or else I had not seen them before,) and returning, sett herself just before me, showing the way to Reding,[1] that I might see her Ornaments, perhaps to' gain the more respect. But her Granam's new Rung sow, had it appeared, would affected me as much. I paid honest John wth money and dram according to contract, and Dismist him, and pray'd Miss to shew me where I must Lodg. Shee conducted me to a parlour in a little back Lento,[2] wch was almost filled wth the bedsted, wch was so high I was forced to climb on a chair to gitt up to ye wretched bed that lay on it; on wch having Stretcht my tired Limbs, and lay'd my head on a Sad-colourd[3] pillow, I began to think on the transactions of ye past day.

Tuesday, October ye third, about 8 in the

---

[1] *In Notes and Queries*, 2d Series, vol 6, p 233, there is an inquiry as to the origin of this phrase, but it is unanswered.

[2] Lean to.

[3] Sombre, dark. "The colours are too sad." Beaumont and Fletcher, *Love's Cure*, Act III, Scene 2, Dyce's edition, vol. IX, p. 151.

morning, I with the Post proceeded forward
without observing any thing remarkable; And
about two, afternoon, Arrived at the Post's second
stage, where the western Post mett[1] him and
exchanged Letters. Here, having called for
something to eat, ye woman bro't in a Twisted
thing like a cable, but something whiter; and
laying it on the bord, tugg'd for life to bring it
into a capacity to spread; wch having wth great
pains accomplished, shee serv'd in a dish of Pork
and Cabage, I suppose the remains of Dinner.
The sause was of a deep Purple, wch I tho't was
boil'd in her dye Kettle; the bread was Indian,
and every thing on the Table service Agreeable
to these. I, being hungry, gott a little down;
but my stomach was soon cloy'd, and what cab-
bage I swallowed serv'd me for a Cudd the whole
day after.

Having here discharged the Ordnary for self
and Guide, (as I understood was the custom,)

[1] The chief post office in Connecticut was New London, and
this post was probably the rider from that place, who exchanged
letters here and then returned to New London. Madam Knight
went with him, and he thus became her "third guide."

4

About Three afternoon went on with my Third
Guide, who Rode very hard: and having crossed
Providence Ferry, we come to a River wch they
Generally Ride thro'.[1] But I dare not venture;
so the Post got a Ladd and Cannoo to carry me
to tother side, and hee rid thro' and Led my hors.
The Cannoo was very small and shallow, so that
when we were in she seem'd redy to take in
water, which greatly terrified mee, and caused
me to be very circumspect, sitting with my
hands fast on each side, my eyes stedy, not

[1] This must have been where the village of Pawtuxet now is.
The route from Boston to New York through Rhode Island followed the shore of the bay and sea very nearly. From Providence
it went through the present villages of Pawtuxet, Apponarg, East
Greenwich, a little west of Wickford, then southerly through
Tower Hill, Wakefield (formerly known as McCoon's Mills), and
then southerly and westerly near the shore by Charlestown and
westerly to Pawcatuc Bridge It was long known as the Pequot
path, road to Pequot and afterwards as the King's or Queen's
Highway and the old Post road, and is throughout of greater
width than the average country roads. A new road through the
present towns of North and South Kingstown leading through
the present village of Kingston was laid out 1703 See Potter's
History of Narragansat. (*R. I. Hist. Soc. Coll*, III, 223). E R. P.

This note and the others with these initials are from the pen of
E R Potter, Esq of Kingston, R. I.

daring so much as to lodg my tongue a hair's
breadth more on one side of my mouth then
tother, nor so much as think on Lott's wife, for
a wry thought would have oversett our wherey;
But was soon put out of this pain, by feeling the
Cannoo on shore, wch I as soon almost saluted with
my feet; and ˙Rewarding my sculler, again
mounted and made the best of our way forwards.
The Rode here was very even and ye day pleasant, it being now near Sunsett. But the Post
told mee we had neer 14 miles to Ride to the
next Stage, (where we were to Lodg.) I askt
him of the rest of the Rode, foreseeing wee must
travail in the night. Hee told mee there was a
bad River we were to Ride thro', wch was so very
firce a hors could sometimes hardly stem it: But
it was but narrow, and wee should soon be over.
I cannot express The concern of mind this relation sett me in: no thoughts but those of the
dang'ros River could entertain my Imagination,
and they were as formidable as varios, still Tor-
menting me with blackest Ideas of my Approch-
ing fate — Sometimes seing myself drowning,
otherwhiles drowned, and at the best like a holy

Sister Just come out of a Spiritual Bath in drip-
ping Garments.

Now was the Glorious Luminary, wth his swift
Coursers arrived at his Stage, leaving poor me
wth the rest of this part of the lower world in
darkness, with which *wee* were soon Surrounded.
The only Glimering we now had was from the
spangled Skies, Whose Imperfect Reflections
rendered every Object formidable.　Each lifeless
Trunk, with its shatter'd Limbs, appear'd an
Armed Enymie; and every little stump like a
Ravenous devourer.　Nor could I so much as
discern my Guide, when at any distance, which
added to the terror.

Thus, absolutely lost in Thought, and dying
with the very thoughts of drowning, I come up
wth the post, who I did not see till even with his
Hors: he told mee he stopt for mee; and wee
Rode on Very deliberatly a few paces, when we
entred a Thickett of Trees and Shrubbs, and I
perceivd by the Hors's going we were on the
descent of a Hill, w^{ch}, as wee come neerer the
bottom, 'twas totaly dark wth the Trees that sur-

rounded it   But I knew by the Going of the Hors wee had entred the water, wch my Guide told mee was the hazzardos River[1] he had told me off; and hee, Riding up close to my Side, Bid me not fear—we should be over Imediatly.   I now ralyed all the Courage I was mistriss of, Knowing that I must either Venture my fate of drowning, or be left like ye Children in the wood. So, as the Post bid me, I gave Reins to my Nagg; and sitting as Stedy as Just before in the Cannoo, in a few minutes got safe to the other side, which hee told mee was the Narragansett country.[2]

[1] This is evidently Mascachuge river, a little south of East Green-wich. The road now by taking from the top of the hill and bridging filling up the hollow between the hills is very tolerable. But within the recollection of the writer the hills were very steep and it was a place dreaded by travelers and teamsters. "A little farther south is Hunt's river, but the description does not at all agree with this   E. R. P.

[2] The Narragansett country, so called from the powerful tribe of that name who originally occupied it, lay between Narragan-sett bay and Pawcatuck river.   It had been claimed both by Con-necticut and by Rhode Island, and these claims had been for many years a cause of strife between those colonies   At one time it was formed into a nominally separate jurisdiction, under the name of The King's Province

Here We found great difficulty in Travailing. the way being very narrow, and on each side the Trees and bushes gave us very unpleasent welcome wth their Branches and bow's, wch wee could not avoid, it being so exceeding dark. My Guide, as before so now, putt on harder than I, wth my weary bones, could follow; so left mee and the way bechind him. Now Returned my distressed aprehensions of the place where I was: the dolesome woods, my Company next to none, Going I knew not whither, and encompased wth Terrifying darkness; The least of which was enough to startle a more Masculine courage. Added to which the Reflections, as in the afternoon of ye day that my Call was very Questionable, wch till then I had not so Prudently as I ought considered. Now, coming to ye foot of a hill, I found great difficulty in ascending; But being got to the Top, was there amply recompenced with the friendly Appearance of the Kind Conductress of the night, Just then Advancing above the Horisontall Line. The Raptures wch the Sight of that fair Planett produced in mee, caus'd mee, for the Moment, to

forgett my present wearyness and past toils;
and Inspir'd me for most of the remaining way
with very divirting thot's, some of which, with
the other Occurances of the day, I reserved to
note down when I should come to my Stage.
My tho'ts on the sight of the moon were to this
purpose ·

Fair Cynthia, all the Homage that I may
Unto a Creature, unto thee I pay;
In Lonesome woods to meet so kind a guide,
To Mee's more worth than all the world beside
Some Joy I felt just now, when safe got or'e
Yon Surly River to this Rugged shore,
Deeming Rough welcomes from these clownish Trees,
Better than Lodgings w̄ Nereidees
Yet swelling fears surprise, all dark appears—
Nothing but Light can disipate those fears
My fainting vitals can't lend strength to say,
But softly whisper, O I wish 'twere day.
The murmer hardly warm'd the Ambient air,
E're thy Bright Aspect rescues from dispair:
Makes the old Hagg her sable mantle loose,
And a Bright Joy do's through my Soul diffuse
The Boistero's Trees now Lend a Passage Free,
And pleasent prospects thou giv'st light to see.

From hence wee kept on, with more ease y^n

before: the way being smooth and even, the night warm and serene, and the Tall and thick Trees at a distance, especially wⁿ the moon glar'd light through the branches, fill'd my Imagination wth the pleasent delusion of a Sump teous citty, fill'd wth famous Buildings and churches, wth their spiring steeples, Balconies, Galleries and I know not what: Granduers wch I had heard of, and wch the stories of foreign countries had given me the Idea of.

> Here stood a Lofty church—there is a steeple,
> And there the Grand Parade—O see the people!
> That Famouse Castle there, were I but nigh,
> To see the mote and Bridg and walls so high—
> They'r very fine! sais my deluded eye.

Being thus agreably entertain'd without a thou't of any thing but thoughts themselves, I on a suden was Rous'd from these pleasing Imaginations, by the Post's sounding his horn, which assured mee hee was arrived at the Stage, where we were to Lodg: and that musick was then most musickall and agreeable to mee.

Being come to mr. Havens',[1] I was very civilly

---

[1] Havens' Tavern, says Mr. Updike in his history of the Episco-

Received, and courteously entertained, in a clean comfortable House; and the Good woman was very active in helping off my Riding cloths, and then ask't what I would eat. I told her I had some Chocolett if shee would prepare it; which with the help of some Milk, and a little clean brass Kettle, she soon effected to my satisfaction. I then betook me to my Apartment, wch was a little Room parted from the Kitchen by a single bord partition; where, after I had noted the Occurrances of the past day, I went to bed, which, tho' pretty hard, Yet neet and handsome. But I could get no sleep, because of

pal church in Narragansett, stood on the site of the house of the late William P. Maxwell, Esq , in North Kingstown, a little south of the well known Devil's Foot rock

It seems rather remarkable that Mrs. Knight does not mention this rock which is partly in the highway and was celebrated among the Indians. Its English name is a translation of the Indian name (See *Records of North Kingston*, 11, 54), and there were strange traditions of the devil's doings connected with it. A short distance south of Havens' was the residence of Lodowick Updike, one of the oldest and best known settlements in the country, settled before the great Indian war of 1675, Mr Updike was then (1704) the proprietor of an immense estate and well known all over the state. (Potter's *Narragansett*, 270, 311, 166) It may perhaps be accounted for by her mode of traveling   E R F

the Clamor of some of the Town tope-ers in next
Room, Who were entred into a strong debate
concerning ye Signifycation of the name of their
Country, (viz.) *Narragunset*. One said it was
named so by ye Indians, because there grew a
Brier there, of a prodigious Highth and bigness,
the like hardly ever known, called by the Indians
Narragansett; And quotes an Indian of so Bar-
berous a name for his Author, that I could not
write it. His Antagonist Replyed no—It was
from a Spring it had its name, wch hee well knew
where it was, which was extreem cold in summer, and as Hott as could be imagined in the
winter, which was much resorted too by the
natives, and by them called Narragansett, (Hott
and Cold,) and that was the originall of their
places name—with a thousand Impertinances
not worth notice, wch He utter'd with such a
Roreing voice and Thundering blows with the
fist of wickedness on the Table, that it peirced
my very head. I heartily fretted, and wish't
'um tongue tyed; but wth as little succes as a
freind of mine once, who was (as shee said)
kept a whole night awake, on a Jorny, by a

country Left, and a Sergent, Insigne and a Dea-
con, contriving how to bring a triangle into a
Square. They kept calling for tother Gill, w^{ch}
while they were swallowing, was some Inter-
mission; But presently, like Oyle to fire,
encreased the flame. I set my Candle on a Chest
by the bed side, and setting up, fell to my old
way of composing my Resentments, in the following manner:

I ask thy Aid, O Potent Rum!

To Charm these wrangling Topers Dum.

Thou hast their Giddy Brains possest—

The man confounded wth the Beast—

And I, poor I, can get no rest.

Intoxicate them with thy fumes:

O still their Tongues till morning comes.

And I know not but my wishes took effect; for
the dispute soon ended wth 'tother Dram; and
so Good night!

Wedensday, Octob^r 4th. About four in the
morning, we set off for Kingston[1] (for so was the
Town called) with a french Docter[2] in our com-

[1] Properly Kingstown. It included the present towns of North
Kingstown, South Kingstown and Exeter. Tower Hill was one of
the earliest settlements and the one probably meant   E. R. P.

[2] A few miles west of the Havens tavern was a settlement of

pany. Hee and ye Post put on very furiously, so that I could not keep up with them, only as now and then they'd stop till they see mee. This Rode was poorly furnished wth accommodations for Travellers, so that we were forced to ride 22 miles by the post's account, but neerer thirty by mine, before wee could bait so much as our Horses, wch I exceedingly complained of. But the post encourag'd mee, by saying wee should be well accommodated anon at mr. Devills,[1] a few miles further. But I questioned whether

French Huguenots One of them,——— Ayrault, was a physician and probably the one mentioned by Mrs Knight (See Potter's *Narragansett*, 105, 109 E. R. P

[1] Davell's Mills, now Cross' Mills in Charlestown Charlestown was formerly a part of the town of Westerly (See Potter's *Narragansett*, 111, 226)

In going from Havens' to Davell's, Mrs Knight passed, but probably before daylight, within a few rods of the Updike house before mentioned. As she crossed Tower hill, she was near the site of Bull's garrison house burnt in the previous Indian war She then came in view of the sea and the famous Point Judith salt ponds Near the present village of Wakefield she passed by the head of these ponds and directly by the side of Sugar Loaf hill, a hill which was known by that name in the time of Roger Williams And farther on was a spring which before 1703 was known as Deadman's spring. A very short distance from Davell's, and near the road, stood an Indian fort well known

we ought to go to the Devil[1] to be helpt out of
affliction. However, like the rest of Deluded
souls that post to ye Infernal denn, Wee made all
posible speed to this Devil's Habitation; where
alliting, in full assurance of good accommodation, wee were going in. But meeting his two
daughters, as I suposed twins, they so neerly
resembled each other, both in features and habit,
and look't as old as the Divel himselfe, and quite
as Ugly, We desired entertainm't, but could
hardly get a word out of 'um, till with our Im-
portunity, telling them our necesity, &c. they
call'd the old Sophister, who was as sparing of
his words as his daughters had bin, and no, or
none, was the reply's hee made us to our
demands. Hee differed only in this from the
old fellow in to'ther Country : hee let us depart.
However, I thought it proper to warn poor
Travailers to endeavour to Avoid falling into cir-

in Indian history. Its remains are remarkable even at this day,
and the place is called Fort Neck These are not mentioned,
probably because she was the only woman in the company and
her mind was intent on the perils of her journey   E R P

[1] This name of Davol or Davell was spelled Devil on old records
of the time of Madam Knight   W. R D.

cumstances like ours, wch at our next Stage I sat
down and did as followeth :

> May all that dread the cruel feind of night
> Keep on, and not at this curs't Mansion light.
> 'Tis Hell; 'tis Hell! and Devills here do dwell.
> Here dwells the Devil—surely this's Hell.
> Nothing but Wants: a drop to cool yo'r Tongue
> Cant be procur'd these cruel Feinds among
> Plenty of horrid Grins and looks sevear,
> Hunger and thirst, But pitty's bannish'd here—
> The Right hand keep, if Hell on Earth you fear !

Thus leaving this habitation of cruelty, we
went forward; and arriving at an Ordinary[1]
about two mile further, found tollerable accomo-
dation. But our Hostes, being a pretty full
mouth'd old creature, entertain'd our fellow
travailer, ye french Doctor, wth Inumirable com-
plaints of her bodily infirmities; and whisper'd
to him so lou'd, that all ye House had as full a
hearing as hee: which was very divirting to y^e
company, (of which there was a great many,)

---

[1] If the "Mr. Divel's" was at Davell's Mill, as we think, this
ordinary might have been at the residence of the Champlins
This family settled there very early and were large proprietors,
and in these days almost every house along the road afforded
entertainment for travelers   E R P.

as one might see by their sneering. But poor
weary I slipt out to enter my mind in my Jornal,
and left my Great Landly with her Talkative
Guests to themselves.

From hence we proceeded (about ten fore-
noon) through the Naragansett country, pretty
Leisurely; and about one afternoon come to
Paukataug River,[1] wch was about two hundred
paces over, and now very high, and no way over
to to'ther side but this. I darid not venture to
Ride thro, my courage at best in such cases but
small, And now at the Lowest Ebb, by reason
of my weary, very weary, hungry and uneasy
Circumstances. So takeing leave of my company,
tho' wth no little Reluctance, that I could not
proceed wth them on my Jorny, Stop at a little
cottage Just by the River, to wait the Waters
falling, wch the old man that lived there said
would be in a little time, and he would conduct

[1]Mr Updike informs me that Jesse Maxon, for many years
Town clerk of Westerly who died a few years ago at an advanced
age told him that the ancient riding over place at Westerly was
five or six rods above the present bridge known as Pawcatuc
Bridge. It was called Sh a's riding over place. A dwelling
house now stands where the old way was   E R P.

me safe over. This little Hutt was one of the wretchedest I ever saw a habitation for human creatures. It was suported with shores enclosed with Clapbords, laid on Lengthways, and so much asunder, that the Light come throu' every where; the doore tyed on wth a cord in ye place of hinges; The floor the bear earth; no windows but such as the thin covering afforded, nor any furniture but a Bedd wth a glass Bottle hanging at ye head on't; an earthan cupp, a small pewter Bason, A Bord wth sticks to stand on, instead of a table, and a block or two in ye corner instead of chairs. The family were the old man, his wife and two Chldren; all and every part being the picture of poverty. Notwithstanding both the Hutt and its Inhabitance were very clean and tydee: to the crossing the Old Proverb, that bare walls make giddy hows-wifes.

I Blest myselfe that I was not one of this misscrable crew, and the Impressions their wretchedness formed in me caused mee on ye very Spott to say:

Tho' Ill at ease, A stranger ard alone,
All my fatigu's shall not extrrt a grone.
These Indigents have hunge with their case;

Then best is wors behalfe than my disease
Then Misirable hutt weh Heat and Cold
Alternately without Repulse do hold;
Their Lodgings thyn and hard, their Indian fare,
Their mean Apparel which the wretches wear,
And their ten thousand ills weh can't be told,
Makes nature er'e 'tis midle age'd look old
When I reflect, my late fatigues do seem
Only a notion or forgotten Dreem.

I had scarce done thinking, when an Indian-
like Animal come to the door, on a creature
very much like himselfe, in mien and feature,
as well as Ragged cloathing; and having 'litt,
makes an Awkerd Scratch wth his Indian shoo,
and a Nodd, sitts on ye block, fumbles out his
black Junk, dipps it in ye Ashes, and presents it
piping hott to his muscheeto's, and fell to suck-
ing like a calf, without speaking, for near a quar-
ter of an hower. At length the old man said
how do's Sarah do? who I understood was the
wretches wife and Daughter to ye old man: he
Replyed—as well as can be expected, &c. So I
remembred the old say, and suposed I knew
Sarah's case. Butt hee being, as I understood,
going over the River, as ugly as hee was, I was

glad to ask him to show me ye way to Saxtons, at Stoningtown; wch he promising, I ventur'd over wth the old man's assistance; who having rewarded to content, with my Tattertailed guide, I Ridd on very slowly thro' Stoningtown, where the Rode was very Stony and uneven.[1] I asked the fellow, as we went, divers questions of the place and way, &c. I being arrived at my country Saxtons,[2] at Stonington, was very well accommodated both as to victuals and Lodging, the only Good of both I had found since my setting out. Here I heard there was an old man and his Daughter to come that way, bound to N. London; and being now destitute of a Guide, gladly waited for them, being in so good a harbour, and accordingly, Thirsday, Octob^r ye 5th, about 3 in the afternoon, I sat forward with

[1] After leaving Pawcatuck river, Madam Knight evidently took the old country road, leading over the hills through the central part of Stonington to the head of Mystic river.—Letter of Miss Caulkins, June 1865.

[2] Capt. Joseph Saxton, who died in 1715, lived some two or three miles east of Mystic. He is described in one document as formerly of Boston. "My Country" undoubtedly means "my countryman" and may indicate that they were both from Boston. — Ibid.

neighbour Polly[1] and Jemima, a Girl about 18
years old, who hee said he had been to fetch
out of the Narragansetts, and said they had
Rode thirty miles that day, on a sory lean jade,
wth only a Bagg under her for a pillion, which
the poor Girl often complain'd was very uneasy.

Wee made Good speed along wch made poor
Jemima make many a sow'r face, the mare being
a very hard trotter; and after many a hearty
and bitter Oh, she at length Low'd out: Lawful
Heart father! this bare mare hurts mee Dingee-
ly, I'me direfull sore I vow, with many words
to that purpose :—poor Child sais Gaffer—she
us't to serve your mother so. I don't care how
mother us't to do, quoth Jemima, in a passionate tone, at which the old man Laught, and
kik't his Jade o' the side, which made her Jolt
ten times harder.

About seven that Evening, we come to New
London Ferry:[2] here, by reason of a very high

[1]This name appears in New London records.

[2]The ferry from Groton to New London had been leased to
Cary Latham for fifty years from March 25th, 1655. The ferriage
was 3d for a passenger, 6d for a horse or great beast and 3d for a
calf or swine. In February 1701-2 the rent of the ferry, after

wind, we mett with great difficulty in getting
over—the Boat tos't exceedingly, and our Horses
capper'd at a very surprizing Rate, and sett us
all in a fright; especially poor Jemima, who
desired her father to say so jack to the Jade, to
make her stand. But the careless parent, taking
no notice of her repeated desires, She Rored out
in a Passionate manner : Pray suth father, Are
you deaf? Say so Jack to the Jade, I tell you.
The Dutiful Parent obey's; saying so Jack, so
Jack, as gravely as if hee'd bin to saying Cate-
chise after Young Miss, who with her fright
look't of all coullers in yᵉ Rain Bow.

Being safely arrived at the house of Mrs.

the expiration of this lease, was appropriated perpetually to the
support of a public grammar school. The Parade, as it was called,
lay at the foot of Court or State street in New London, and
from the eastern part of the Parade the coast originally turned to
the west, and was bordered by a strip of sand beach. At the
head of this beach were the ferry stairs and the old town landing
place, where in 1703 was built the town wharf. The railroad
ferry by which travelers from Boston, by the way of Stonington,
now cross on their way to New Haven and New York, lies farther south, even on the New London side. Down to 1800 the
ferry boat was a scow, propelled by sails and oars. A rough
passage, such as Madam Knight describes, was nothing unusual.—
Miss Caulkins' *History of New London*, 89, 134, 180, 102.

Prentices[1] in N. London, I treated neighbour
Polly and daughter for their divirting company,
and bid them farewell; and between nine and
ten at night waited on the Rev[d] Mr. Gurdon
Saltonstall,[2] minister of the town, who kindly
Invited me to Stay that night at his house,
where I was very handsomely and plentifully
treated and Lodg'd; and made good the Great
Character I had before heard concerning him:

[1] The old Prentis homestead was near the north end of Main
street, where is now the old Deshon house. The first John Prentis died in 1691, and his relict, a third wife whom he had married
late in life, survived him many years and kept a house of entertainment. More than one reference can be found to the tavern
of the widow Prentis — Miss Caulkins' letter

[2] Gurdon Saltonstall, eldest son of Nathaniel Saltonstall of
Haverhill, Mass, was born March 27, 1666; was graduated at
Harvard where he was a distinguished scholar, and was ordained
at New London in 1691 He became very celebrated as a preacher.
On the death of Fitz John Winthrop in 1707, he was chosen
governor of Connecticut, and he continued in that office till his
death in 1724. ' Who did not admire his consummate wisdom,
profound learning, his dexterity in business and indefatigable ap-
plication, his intimate acquaintance with men and things and his
superior genius " — (*Funeral Discourse* by Rev. Eliphalet Adams.)
Mr Saltonstall's house was next to that of Mrs Prentis, so that
Madam Knight had not far to go in making her late evening

viz. that he was the most affable, courteous
Genero's and best of men.

Friday, Octo^r 6th.   I got up very early, in
Order to hire somebody to go with mee to New
Haven, being in great parplexity at the thoughts
of proceeding alone; which my most hospitable
entertainer observing, himself went, and soon
return'd wth a young Gentleman of the town,
who he could confide in to Go with mee; and
about eight this morning, wth Mr. Joshua Wheeler[1] my new Guide, takeing leave of this worthy
Gentleman, Wee advanced on toward Seabrook.
The Rodes all along this way are very bad, Incumbred wth Rocks and mountainos passages,
wch were very disagreeable to my tired carcass;
but we went on with a moderate pace wch made
ye Journey more pleasent.   But after about
eight miles Rideing, in going over a Bridge[2] under

[1] Below the houses of Mr. Saltonstall and of Mrs. Prentis and
on the opposite side of the way stood the Wheeler house   Mr.
Saltonstall therefore *soon* returned   John Wheeler was one of
the early shipping merchants of New London   His son Joshua,
born in 1681, was undoubtedly Madam Knight's guide — *Ibid.*

[2] This river must be the Niantic   At the crossing, known as
Rope Ferry, there was no bridge until long after Madam Knight's

wch the River Run very swift, my hors stum-
bled, and very narrowly 'scaped falling over into
the water; wch extreemly frightened mee. But
through God's Goodness I met with no harm,
and mounting agen, in about half a miles Rideing, come to an ordinary, were well entertained
by a woman of about seventy and vantage, but
of as Sound Intellectuals as one of seventeen.
Shee entertain'd Mr. Wheeler wth some passages
of a Wedding awhile ago at a place hard by,
the Brides-Groom being about her Age or something above, Saying his Children was dredfully
against their fathers marrying wch shee con-
demned them extreemly for.

From hence wee went pretty briskly forward,
and arriv'd at Saybrook ferry about two of the

day She must therefore have crossed at the bridge near "River
head," which by the present road, is less than six miles from
New London. This road is an old route, but may not have been
opened as early as 1704. It is probable that Madam Knight went
out on the old road that leads by Miss Latimer's, four miles; then
turned west into the Douglas road, which at the end of two miles
would bring her to a narrow, rugged road, (originally an old Indian trail,) that goes directly to the head of the river • She would
thus have had her full eight miles of "*very bad Rodes Incumbred
with Rocks and mountainos passages*"— *Ibid*

Clock afternoon; and crossing it, wee call'd at an Inn to Bait, (foreseeing we should not have such another Opportunity till we come to Killingsworth.) Landlady come in, with her hair about her ears, and hands at full pay scratching. Shee told us shee had some mutton wch shee would broil, wch I was glad to hear; But I supose forgot to wash her scratchers; in a little time shee brot it in; but it being pickled, and my Guide said it smelt strong of head sause, we left it, and p^{d} sixpence a piece for our Dinners, wch was only smell.

So wee putt forward with all speed, and about seven at night come to Killingsworth, and were tollerably well with Travillers fare, and Lodgd there that night.

˙ Saturday, Oct. 7th, we sett out early in the Morning, and being something unaquainted wth the way, having ask't it of some wee mett, they told us wee must Ride a mile or two and turne down a Lane on the Right hand; and by their Direction wee Rode on, but not Yet comeing to ye turning, we mett a Young fellow and ask't him how farr it was to the Lane which turn'd down towards Guilford. Hee said wee must Ride a little further, and turn down by the Corner of uncle Sams Lott. My Guide vented his Spleen at the Lubber; and we soon after came into the Rhode, and keeping still on, without any thing further Remarkabell, about two a clock afternoon we arrived at New Haven, where I was received with all Posible Respects and civility. Here I discharged Mr. Wheeler with a reward to his satisfaction, and took some time to rest after so long and toilsome a Journey; And Inform'd myselfe of the manners and customs of the place. and at the same time employed myselfe in the afair I went there upon.

They are Govern'd by the same Laws as wee in Boston, (or little differing.) thr'out this whole Colony of Connecticot,[1] And much the same way of Church Government. and many of them good, Sociable people, and I hope Religious too · but a little too much Independant in their principalls,[2]

[1] "The earliest code in Connecticut, related only to capital offences. Adopted a year later than the Massachusetts Body of Liberties, it is in great part a verbal copy from that instrument." — Palfrey's *New England*, II, 31.

[2] "The habits of thought of this fraternity," (the settlers of

7

and, as I have been told, were formerly in their
Zeal very Riggid in their Administrations towards such as their Lawes made Offenders, even
to a harmless Kiss[1] or Innocent merriment among
Young people.   Whipping[2] being a frequent and
counted an easy Punishment, about wch as other
Crimes, the Judges were absolute[3] in their Sent-
ances.   They told mee a pleasant story about
a pair of Justices in those parts, wch I may not
omit the relation of.

New Haven,) "led them to carry out to its last results the idea
which had fascinated so many thinking persons at that period, of
finding in scripture a special rule for every thing of the nature of
civil as well as of eccleasiastical order and administration."—Palfrey's *New England*, I, 528.

[1] The tradition of this strictness may have supplied a hint for
one of the, so called, "Blue Laws." "No woman shall kiss her
child on the Sabbath or Fast day." And at least it is evident
from this Journal that the story of some New Haven legislation
against kissing had existed long before 1781 when Samuel Peters
published his history of Connecticut, in which, (as it is said,) the
fiction of the "Blue Laws" first appeared.—Kingsley's *Historical
Discourse*, 84.

[2] "Defamation had in some instances been punished by fine, repeated scourgings and imprisonment"—Trumbull's *History of
Connecticut*, I, 177.

[3] This probably refers to the absence in earlier times of the
trial by Jury and the want of any body of statutes, the Mosaic

A negro Slave belonging to a man in ye Town, stole a hogs head from his master, and gave or sold it to an Indian, native of the place. The Indian sold it in the neighbourhood. and so the theft was found out. Thereupon the Heathen was Seized, and carried to the Justices House to be Examined. But his worship (it seems) was gone into the feild, with a Brother in office, to gather in his Pompions. Whither the malefactor is hurried, And Complaint made, and satisfaction in the name of Justice demanded. Their Worships cann't proceed in form without a Bench: whereupon they Order one to be Imediately erected, which, for want of fitter materials, they made with pompions — which being finished, down setts their Worships, and the Malefactor call'd, and by the Senior Justice Interrogated after the following manner. You Indian why did You steal from this man? You sho'dn't do so — it's a Grandy wicked thing to steal. Hol't Hol't cryes Justice Junr Brother, You speak

law being established as the rule to all courts, until it should be "branched out into particulars." "Until this time punishments in many instances had been uncertain and arbitrary. They had been left wholly to the discretion of the court "—Trumbull, i, 177.

negro to him. I'le ask him. You sirrah, why did
You steal this man's Hoggshead? Hoggshead,
(replys the Indian,) me no stomany.[1] No? says
his Worship; and pulling off his hatt, Patted his
own head with his hand, sais. Tatapa[2]—You,
Tatapa—you; all one this. Hoggshead all one
this Hah! says Netop,[3] now me stomany that.
Whereupon the Company fell into a great fitt of
Laughter, even to Roreing. Silence is comand-
ed, but to no effect. for they continued perfectly
Shouting. Nay, sais his worship, in an angry
tone, if it be so, *take mee off the Bench.*

Their Diversions in this part of the Country
are on Lecture days and Training days mostly
on the former there is Riding from town to
town.

And on training dayes The Youth divert
themselves by Shooting at the Target, as they
call it, (but it very much resembles a pillory,)

[1] *Query* Corruption of *understand*

[2] *Tatta pitch* is said to mean· I cannot tell — Roger Williams
Key, *Mass Historical Collections*, 1st series, v, 89

[3] " What cheer Netop, is the general salutation of all English
to them *Netop* is friend "—Roger Williams Key, *Mass Historical
Collections*, 1st series, III 207

where hee that hitts neerest the white has some
yards of Red Ribbin presented him, wch being
tied to his hattband, the two ends streeming
down his back, he is Led away in Triumph, w^th
great applause, as the winners of the Olympiack
Games. They generally marry very young:
the males oftener as I am told under twentie
than above; they generally make public wed-
ings, and have a way something singular (as
they say) in some of them, viz. Just before
Joyning hands the Bridegroom quitts the place,
who is soon followed by the Bridesmen, and as
it were, dragg'd back to duty — being the reverse
to ye former practice among us, to steal m' Pride.

There are great plenty of Oysters all along
by the sea side, as farr as I Rode in the Collony,
and those very good. And they Generally lived
very well and comfortably in their famelies.
But too Indulgent (especially ye farmers) to
their slaves · sufering too great familiarity from
them, permitting y^m to sit at Table and eat with
them, (as they say to save time.) and into the dish
goes the black hoof as freely as the white hand.
They told me that there was a farmer lived nere

the Town where I lodgd who had some differ
ence wth his slave, concerning something the
master had promised him and did not punctualy
perform; wch caused some hard words between
them; But at length they put the matter to
Arbitration and Bound themselves to stand to
the award of such as they named — wch done,
the Arbitrators Having heard the Allegations
of both parties, Order the master to pay 40^s to
black face, and acknowledge his fault. And so
the matter ended : the poor master very honest-
ly standing to the award.[1]

There are every where in the Towns as I
passed, a Number of Indians the Natives of the
Country, and are the most salvage of all the
salvages of that kind that I had ever Seen :
little or no care taken (as I heard upon enquiry)
to make them otherwise. They have in some
places Landes of theire owne, and Govern'd by
Law's of their own making ;— they marry many
wives and at pleasure put them away, and on
the ye least dislike or fickle humor, on either

[1] From this little incident it may be seen that, even at this early
time, slavery, in Connecticut, was a very different thing from
the system which has existed in the southern part of our country

side, saying *stand away* to one another is a
sufficient Divorce.   And indeed those uncomely
Stand aways are too much in Vongue among the
English in this (Indulgent Colony) as their
Records plentifully prove, and that on very tri-
vial matters, of which some have been told me,
but are not proper to be Related by a Female
pen. tho some of that foolish sex have had too
large a share in the story.[1]

If the natives committ any crime on their
own precints among themselves, ye English
takes no Cognezens of.   But if on the English

[1] This facility for obtaining divorce may have arisen from the
degradation of marriage to a mere civil contract entered into before a magistrate   It was certainly in striking contrast with the
strictness which could lead a grand jury to present a young man
and woman "for sitting together on the Lord's day under an apple
tree"   Unfortunately the same facility has continued to the present time in this "indulgent colony."   Courts can divorce for a
desertion of three years, for habitual drunkenness and for such
*misconduct as permanently destroys the happiness of the other party
and defeats the purposes of the marriage relation*   While a standing
committee of every legislature was until recently at the service
of such persons as could not meet even the easy requirements
for judicial relief   And these divorces were all *a vinculo*   The
present governor of that state officially speaks of these practices
as   "a scandal upon our reputation and a reproach to our mor-
als and our religion"

ground, they are punishable by our Laws. They mourn for their Dead by blacking their faces, and cutting their hair, after an Awkerd and frightfull manner; But can't bear You should mention the names of their dead Relations to them : they trade most for Rum, for wch they^d hazzard their very lives; and the English fit them Generally as well, by seasoning it plentifully with water.

They give the title of merchant to every trader; who Rate their Goods according to the time and spetia they pay in. viz. Pay, mony. Pay as mony, and trusting. *Pay* is Grain, Pork, Beef. &c. at the prices sett by the General Court that Year;[1] *mony* is pieces of Eight, Ryalls, or Boston or Bay shillings (as they call them.) or Good hard money, as sometimes silver coin is termed by them; also Wampom, vizt Indian beads wch serves for change. *Pay as mony* is provisions, as afores^d one Third cheaper then

[1] In laying taxes, or rates, the general court often provided that they might be paid in wheat or certain other agricultural products, at specified prices. For instances see *Connecticut Public Records* (1655-77) 269, 322.

as the Assembly or Gene' Court setts it; and *Trust* as they and the merch' agree for time.

Now, when the buyer comes to ask for a comodity, sometimes before the merchant answers that he has it, he sais, *is Your pay redy?* Perhaps the Chap Reply's Yes: what do You pay in? say's the merchant. The buyer having answered, then the price is set; as suppose he wants a sixpenny knife, in pay it is 12d — in pay as money eight pence, and hard money its own price, viz. 6d. It seems a very Intricate way of trade and what Lex Mercatoria had not thought of.

Being at a merchants house, in comes a tall country fellow wth his alfogeos[1] full of Tobacco; for they seldom Loose their Cudd, but keep Chewing and Spitting as long as they'r eyes are open — he advanc't to the midle of the Room, makes an Awkward Nodd, and spitting a Large deal of Aromatick Tincture, he gave a scrape with his shovel like shoo, leaving a small shovel

[1] This word is probably a corruption of the Spanish *alforja*, saddlebag, portmanteau, or of the Portuguese *alforges* (plural), a wallet or bag, usually for provisions; and it here seems to mean a tobacco pouch.

full of dirt on the floor, made a full stop, Hugging his own pretty Body with his hands under his arms, Stood staring rown'd him, like a Catt let out of a Baskett. At last, like the creature Balaam Rode on, he opened his mouth and said: have You any Ribinen for Hatbands to sell I pray? The Questions and Answers about the pay being past, the Ribin is bro't and opened. Bumpkin Simpers, cryes its confounded Gay I vow; and beckning to the door, in comes Jone Tawdry, dropping about 50 curtsees, and stands by him: hee shows her the Ribin. *Law You,* sais shee, *its right Gent,* do You take it, *tis dreadfull pretty.* Then she enquires, *hare You any hood silk I pray?* wch being brought and bought, Have You any *thred silk to sew it wth* says shee, wch being accomodated wth they Departed. They Generaly stand after they come in a great while speachless, and sometimes dont say a word till they are askt what they want, which I Impute to the Awe they stand in of the merchants, who they are constantly almost Indebted too; and must take what they bring without Liberty to choose for themselves; but they serve them as

well, making the merchants stay long enough
for their pay.

We may Observe here the great necessity and
bennifitt both of Education and Conversation;
for these people have as Large a portion of
mother witt, and sometimes a Larger, than those
who have bin brought up in Citties; But for
want of emprovements, Render themselves almost Ridiculos, as above.[1] I should be glad if
they would leave such follies, and am sure all
that Love Clean Houses (at least) would be glad
on't too.

They are generaly very plain in their dress,
throuout all ye Colony, as I saw, and follow one
another in their modes; that You may know
where they belong, especially the women, meet
them where you will.

Their Cheif Red Letter day is St. Election,[2]
wch is annualy Observed according to Charter,
to choose their Goven^r: a blessing they can

[1] From the tone of this sentiment one might think that Madam
Knight had already commenced her school keeping

[2] "It was first the custom and afterwards the order that the
ministers of the gospel should preach a sermon on the day appointed for the choice of civil rulers." — Bancroft's *Hist.* iii, 69.

never be thankfull enough for, as they will find
if ever it be their hard fortune to loose it.[1]   The
present Govenor in Conecticott is the Hon[ble] John
Winthrop, Esq.[2] A Gentleman of an Ancient and
Honourable Family, whose Father[3] was Govenor here sometime before, and his Grand father
had bin Gov[r] of the Massachusetts.   This gentleman is a very curteous and afable person,
much Given to Hospitality, and has by his Good
services Gain'd the affections of the people as
much as any who had bin before him in that
post.

Dec[r] 6th.   Being by this time well Recruited
and rested after my Journy, my business lying

[1] The allusion here is to the proceedings on the part of Lord
Cornbury and Gov Dudley to take away the Connecticut charter ;
in which they were favored by the difficulties arising out of the
Liveen will — Bancroft's *Hist* III, 70   Trumbull's *Hist* 1, 417.
Miss Caulkins' *New London*, chap XV.

[2] Major General Fitz-John Winthrop was elected Governor of
Connecticut in 1698.   He was born in 1638, and died at Boston
in 1707.   He had been the Commander-in-chief of the unfortunate
expedition against Canada in 1690   Perhaps the ill-will felt towards him in New York on account of that failure increased his
popularity in Connecticut

[3] John Winthrop " the younger "

unfinished by some concerns at New York
depending thereupon, my Kinsman, Mr. Thomas Trowbridge[1] of New Haven, must needs
take a Journy there before it could be accomplished, I resolved to go there in company w[th]
him, and a man of the town w[ch] I engaged to
wait on me there. Accordingly, Dec. 6th we set
out from New Haven, and about 11 same morning came to Stratford ferry[2]; w[ch] crossing, about
two miles on the other side Baited our horses
and would have eat a morsell ourselves, But the
Pumpkin and Indian mixt Bred[3] had such an
Aspect, and the Bare-legg'd Punch so awkerd or
rather Awfull a sound, that we left both, and
proceeded forward, and about seven at night
come to Fairfield, where we met with good entertainment and Lodg'd; and early next morning set forward to Norowalk,[4] from its halfe
Indian name *North-walk*, when about 12 at noon

---

[1] Thomas Trowbridge, son of Thomas and of Sarah Rutherford,
his wife, born Feb 14, 1664. Savage's *Genealogical Dictionary.*

[2] See *Conn. Public Records* (1655-77) 136, 253.

[3] Bread made of Indian meal with a mixture of pumpkin.

[4] Narawauk, now Norwalk, has the same origin and meaning
with Norridgewock; from *nara*, still water below falls, *wampi*
clean, *ack*, locative — *Historical Magazine*, IX, 91.

we arrived, and Had a Dinner of Fryed Venison,
very savoury. Landlady wanting some pepper
in the seasoning, bid the Girl hand her the spice
in the little *Gay* cupp on ye shelfe. From hence
we Hasted towards Rye, walking and Leading
our Horses neer a mile together, up a prodigios
high Hill; and so Riding till about nine at
night, and there arrived and took up our Lodgings at an ordinary, wch a French family kept.
Here being very hungry, I desired a fricasee w^ch
the Frenchman undertakeing, managed so con-
trary to my notion of Cookery, that I hastned
to Bed superless; And being shewd the way up
a pair of stairs wch had such a narrow passage
that I had almost stopt by the Bulk of my Body,
But arriving at my apartment found it to be a
little Lento Chamber furnisht amongst other
Rubbish with a High Bedd and a Low one, a
Long Table, a Bench and a Bottomless chair, —
Little Miss went to scratch up my Kennell w^ch
Russelled as if shee'd bin in the Barn amongst
the Husks, and supose such was the contents of
the tickin — nevertheless being exceeding weary,
down I laid my poor Carkes (never more tired)

and found my Covering as scanty as my Bed
was hard. Annon I heard another Russelling
noise in Y° Room—called to know the matter
— Little miss said shee was making a bed for
the men; who, when they were in Bed, complained their leggs lay out of it by reason of its
shortness — my poor bones complained bitterly
not being used to such Lodgings, and so did the
man who was with us; and poor I made but
one Grone, which was from the time I went to
bed to the time I Riss, which was about three
in the morning, Setting up by the Fire till Light,
and having discharged our ordinary wch was as
dear as if we had had far Better fare — we took
our leave of Monsier and about seven in the
morn come to New Rochell a french town, where
we had a good Breakfast. And in the strength
of that about an how'r before sunsett got to
York. Here I applyd myself to Mr. Burroughs,[1]
a merchant to whom I was recommended by my
Kinsman Capt. Prout, and received great Civil-

[1] Probably Thomas Burroughs, a prominent Merchant. Valentine's *History of New York*, 219 In a census taken in 1703 his
name appears as a resident of Dock Ward. *Documentary History
of N. Y.*, I, 611 He was a vestryman of Trinity church.

ities from him and his spouse, who were now both Deaf but very agreeable in their Conversation, Diverting me with pleasant stories of their knowledge in Brittan from whence they both come, one of which was above the rest very pleasant to me viz. my Lord Darcy had a very extravagant Brother who had mortgaged what Estate hee could not sell, and in good time dyed leaving only one son. Him his Lordship (having none of his own) took and made him Heir of his whole Estate, which he was to receive at the death of his Aunt. He and his Aunt in her widowhood held a right understanding and lived as become such Relations, shee being a discreat Gentlewoman and he an Ingenios Young man. One day Hee fell into some Company though far his inferiors, very freely told him of the Ill circumstances his fathers Estate lay under, and the many Debts he left unpaid to the wrong of poor people with whom he had dealt. The Young gentleman was put out of countenance — no way hee could think of to Redress himself — his whole dependance being on the Lady his Aunt, and how to speak to her he knew not — Hee

went home, sat down, to dinner and as usual
sometimes with her when the Chaplain was
absent, she desired him to say Grace, wch he did
after this manner:

> Pray God in Mercy take my Lady Darcy
> Unto his Heavenly Throne,
> That Little John may live like a man,
> And pay every man his own.

The prudent Lady took no present notice, But
finishd dinner, after wch having sat and talk't
awhile (as Customary) He Riss, took his Hatt
and Going out she desired him to give her leave
to speak to him in her Clossett, Where being
come she desired to know why hee prayed for
her Death in the manner aforesaid, and what
part of her deportment towards him merritted
such desires. Hee Reply'd, none at all, But he
was under such disadvantages that nothing but
that could do him service, and told her how he
had been affronted as above, and what Impressions it had made upon him. The Lady made
him a gentle reprimand that he had not inform-
ed her after another manner, Bid him see what
his father owed and he should have money to

pay it to a penny, And always to lett her know his wants and he should have a redy supply. The Young Gentleman charm'd with his Aunts Discrete management, Beggd her pardon and accepted her kind offer and retrieved his fathers Estate, &c. and said Hee hoped his Aunt would never dye, for shee had done better by him than hee could have done for himself.—Mr. Burroughs went with me to Vendue where I bought about 100 Rheem of paper wch was retaken in a fly boat from Holland and sold very Reasonably here — some ten, some Eight shillings per Rheem by the Lott wch was ten Rheem in a Lott. And at the Vendue I made a great many acquaintances amongst the good women of the town, who curteosly invited me to their houses and generously entertained me.

The Cittic of New York is a pleasant well compacted place, situated on a Commodius River wch is a fine harbour for shipping. The Buildings Brick Generaly, very stately and high, though not altogether like ours in Boston. The Bricks in some of the Houses are of divers Coullers and laid in Checkers, being glazed look very agreeable. The inside of them are neat to admiration, the wooden work, for only the walls are plasterd, and the Sumers and Gist[1] are plained and kept very white scowr'd as so is all the partitions if made of Bords. The fire places have no Jambs (as ours have) But the Backs run flush with the walls, and the Hearth is of Tyles and is as farr out into the Room at the Ends as before the fire, w[ch] is Generally Five foot in the Low'r rooms, and the peice over where the mantle tree should be is made as ours with Joyners work, and as I supose is fasten'd to iron rodds inside. The House where the Vendue was, had Chimney Corners like ours, and they and the hearths were laid wth the finest tile that I ever see, and the stair cases laid all with white tile which is ever clean,[2] and so are

[1] Summers and joist. The summer, a word not now in very common use, was a central beam supporting the joist, such as is now sometimes called the bearing-beam.

[2] The tiles were set into the wall, forming, as it were, a continuous border, or row, of the width of one tile (or perhaps sometimes of more), close to the upper line of the staircase.

The Coeymans house, standing on the bank of the Hudson, just north of the village of Coeymans, still shows most of these peculiarities of building mentioned by Madam Knight. — the

the walls of the Kitchen wch had a Brick floor.
They were making Great preparations to Re-
ceive their Govenor, Lord Cornbury from the
Jerseys, and for that End raised the militia to
Gard him on shore to the fort.[1]

They are Generaly of the Church of England
and have a New England Gentleman[2] for their
minister, and a very fine church set out with all
Customary requsites. There are also a Dutch[3]
and Divers Conventicles as they call them, viz.

staircase laid with tiles; no plaster except on the walls; and
heavy floor-timbers, strengthened at the ends by solid knees,
planed and "kept very white scoured."

[1] On the block between Bowling Green, Whitehall, Bridge and
State streets —Valentine's *History of New York*, 28.

[2] William Vesey, previously "a dissenting preacher on Long
Island He had received his education in Harvard under that
rigid Independent, Increase Mather, and was sent from thence by
him to confirm the minds of those who had removed for their
convenience from New England to this Province. * * *
But Col. Fletcher, who saw into his design, took off Mr. Vesey
by an invitation to this Living, * * * and Mr Vesey
returned from England in Priest's orders." —*Documentary History
of New York*, III, 438.

[3] The Reformed Dutch Church built in 1693 in what is now
Exchange Place. — Greenleaf's *History of N. Y. Churches*, 11.

Baptist,[1] Quakers,[2] &c. They are not strict in
keeping the Sabbath as in Boston and other
places where I had bin, But seem to deal with
great exactness as farr as I see or Deall with.
They are sociable to one another and Curteos
and Civill to strangers and fare well in their
houses. The English go very fasheonable in
their dress. Dut the Dutch, especially the mid-
dling sort, differ from our women, in their habitt
go loose, were French muches wch are like a
Capp and a head band in one, leaving their ears
bare, which are sett out wth Jewells of a large
size and many in number. And their fingers
hoop't with Rings, some with large stones in
them of many Coullers as were their pendants
in their ears, which You should see very old
women wear as well as Young.

They have Vendues very frequently and

---

[1] Greenleaf however gives 1799 as the first Baptist preaching,
that of Wickenden. A petition of Nicholas Eyres states that in
1715 his house was registered for an anabaptist meeting house. —
D cumentary History of New York, iii, 480.'

[2] The first Friends' Meeting House, a small frame building,
standing on Little Green Street, is said to have been erected in
1696 or 1703 — Greenleaf, 116

make their Earnings very well by them, for they
treat with good Liquor Liberally, and the Cust.
omers Drink as Liberally and Generally pay
for't as well, by paying for that which they Bidd
up Briskly for, after the sack has gone plentifully about, tho' sometimes good penny worths
are got there.   Their Diversions in the Winter
is Riding Sleys about three or four Miles out of
Town, where they have Houses of entertainment at a place called the Bowery,[1] and some go
to friends Houses who handsomely treat them.
Mr. Burroughs carry'd his spouse and Daughter
and myself out to one Madame Dowes. a Gentlewoman that lived at a farm House, who gave
us a handsome Entertainment of five or six
Dishes and choice Beer and metheglin, Cyder,
&c. all which she said was the produce of her
farm.   I believe we mett 50 or 60 slays that
day—they fly with great swiftness and some
are so furious that they'le turn out of the path

[1] "A small tavern stood on the banks of the Harlem river.
This tavern was the occasional point of excursion for riding
parties from the City and was known as the ' Wedding Place.'
One or two small taverns were on the road between the town and
the Bowery " — Valentine's *History of New York*, 69

for none except a Loaden Cart. Nor do they
spare for any diversion the place affords, and sociable to a degree, they'r Tables being as free to
their Naybours as to themselves.

Having here transacted the affair I went
upon and some other that fell in the way, after
about a fortnight's stay there I left New York
with no Little regrett. and Thursday, Dec. 21,
set out for New Haven wth my Kinsman Trowbridge, and the man that waited on me about
one afternoon, and about three come to half-way
house about ten miles out of town, where we
Baited and went forward, and about 5 come to
Spiting Devil, Else Kings bridge, where they
pay three pence for passing over with a horse,
which the man that keeps the Gate set up at the
end of the Bridge receives.

We hoped to reach the french town and Lodg
there that night, but unhapily lost our way
about four miles short, and being overtaken by
a great storm of wind and snow which set full
in our faces about dark, we were very uneasy.
But meeting one Gardner who lived in a Cottage thereabout, offered us his fire to set by,

having but one poor Bedd, and his wife not well,
&c. or he would go to a House with us, where
he thought we might be better accommodated
—thither we went, But a surly old shee Creature, not worthy the name of woman, who
would hardly let us go into her Door, though
the weather was so stormy none but shee would
have turnd out a Dogg. But her son whose
name was gallop, who lived Just by Invited us
to his house and shewed me two pair of stairs,
viz one up the loft and tother up the Bedd, w^{ch}
was as hard as it was high, and warmed it with
a hott stone at the feet. I lay very uncomfort-
ably, insomuch that I was so very cold and sick
I was forced to call them up to give me something to warm me. They had nothing but milk
in the house, wch they Boild, and to make it better sweetened wth molasses, which I not knowing or thinking oft till it was down and coming
up agen wch it did in so plentifull a manner that
my host was soon paid double for his portion,
and that in specia. But I believe it did me
service in Cleering my stomach. "So after this
sick and weary night at East Chester, (a very

miserable poor place,) the weather being now fair, Friday the 22ᵈ Dec. we set out for New Ro- chell, where being come we had good Entertain- ment and Recruited ourselves very well. This is a very pretty place well compact, and good handsome houses, Clean, good and passable Rodes, and situated on a Navigable River, abun- dance of land well fined and Cleerd all along as wee passed, which caused in me a Love to the place, wᶜʰ I could have been content to live in it. Here wee Ridd over a Bridge made of one entire stone of such a Breadth that a cart might pass with safety, and to spare—it lay over a passage cutt through a Rock to convey water to a mill not farr off. Here are three fine Taverns with- in call of each other, very good provision for Travailers.

Thence we travailed through Merrinak,[1] a neet, though little place, wᵗʰ a navigable River before it, one of the pleasantest I ever see— Here were good Buildings, Especialy one, a very fine seat, wᶜʰ they told me was Col. Heth-

[1] Mamaroneck

coats,[1] who I had heard was a very fine Gentleman. From hence we come to Hors Neck,[2]
where wee Baited, and they told me that one
Church of England parson officiated in all these
three towns once every Sunday in turns throughout the Year; and that they all could but poorly
maintaine him, which they grudg'd to do, being
a poor and quarelsome crew as I understand by
our Host; their Quarelling about their choice
of Minister, they chose to have none—But
caused the Government to send this Gentleman
to them. Here wee took leave of York Government, and Descending the Mountainos passage
that almost broke my heart in ascending before,
we come to Stamford, a well compact Town, but
miserable meeting house, wch we passed, and
thro' many and great difficulties, as Bridges
which were exceeding high and very tottering
and of vast Length, steep and Rocky Hills and
precipices, (Buggbears to a fearful female travailer.) About nine at night we come to Norr-

[1] Col. Caleb Heathcote, of Scarsdale Manor. See *Colonial History of New York; passim*
[2] West Greenwich.

walk, having crept over a timber of a Broken Bridge[1] about thirty foot long, and perhaps fifty to ye water. I was exceeding tired and cold when we come to our Inn, and could get nothing there but poor entertainment, and the Impertinant Bable of one of the worst of men, among many others of which our Host made one, who, had he bin one degree Impudenter, would have outdone his Grandfather. And this I think is the most perplexed night I have yet had. From hence, Saturday, Dec. 23, a very cold and windy day, after an Intolerable night's Lodging, wee hasted forward only observing in our way the Town to be situated on a Navigable river wth indiferent Buildings and people more refind than in some of the Country towns wee had passed, tho' vicious enough, the Church and Tavern being next neighbours. Having Ridd thro a difficult River[2] wee come to Fairfield

[1] A committee was appointed by the town of Norwalk February, 20, 1694-5 to "take an exact view of the Bridge over Norwalk River and to repaire the same, *eyther by erecting a new bridge*, or by repairing the old " — Hall's *Norwalk Records*, 88.

[2] Probably the Saugatuck

where wee Baited and were much refreshed as
well with the Good things wch gratified our ap-
petites as the time took to rest our wearied
Limbs, wch Latter I employed in enquiring concerning the Town and manners of the people,
&c.   This is a considerable town, and filld as
they say with wealthy people — have a spacious
meeting house and good Buildings.   But the
Inhabitants are Litigious, nor do they well agree
with their minister, who (they say) is a very
worthy Gentleman.[1]

They have aboundance of sheep, whose very
Dung brings them great gain, with part of which
they pay their Parsons sallery, And they Grudg
that, prefering their Dung before their minister.
They Lett out their sheep at so much as they
agree upon for a night ; the highest Bidder
always caries them, And they will sufficiently
Dung a Large quantity of Land before morning.

[1] Joseph Webb, ordained at Fairfield in 1694   Even before his
time the General Court appointed a committee " to improve there
best abillities to settle an accomadation between the people and
minister of Fayrefeild, that so if it be the will of God Mr. Wake-
man may continue in his worke there."—*Conn. Public Records*, 240.

But were once Bitt by a sharper who had them
a night and sheared them all before morning —
From hence we went to Stratford, the next
Town, in which I observed but few houses, and
those not very good ones. But the people that
I conversed with were civill and good natured.
Here we staid till late at night, being to cross a
Dangerous River ferry, the River[1] at that time
full of Ice; but after about four hours waiting
with great difficulty wee got over. My fears
and fatigues prevented my here taking any particular observation. Being got to Milford, it
being late in the night, I could go no further;
my fellow travailer going forward, I was invited
to Lodg at Mrs. ———, a very kind and civill
Gentlewoman, by whom I was handsomely and
kindly entertained till the next night. The
people here go very plain in their apparel (more
plain than I had observed in the towns I had
passed) and seem to be very grave and serious.
They told me there was a singing Quaker[2] lived

[1] The Housatonic.

[2] "One Case and one Banks, two lewd men called *singing Quakers*, coming through the Colony, singing and dancing, accompa-

there, or at least had a strong inclination to be so, His Spouse not at all affected that way. Some of the singing Crew come there one day to visit him, who being then abroad, they sat down (to the woman's no small vexation) Humming and singing and groneing after their conjuring way—Says the woman are you singing quakers? Yea says They—Then take my squalling Brat of a child here and sing to it says she for I have almost split my throat wth singing to him and cant get the Rogue to sleep. They took this as a great Indignity, and mediately departed. Shaking the dust from their Heels left the good woman and her Child among the number of the wicked.

This is a Seaport place and accomodated with a Good Harbour, But I had not opportunity to make particular observations because it was Sabbath day—This Evening.[1]

nied with a number of women to assist them in their musical exercises and especially to proclaim how their lips dropped with myrrh and honey."—Trumbull's *Hist. Conn.*, II, 36, note.

[1] It was Saturday, and, according to the well known Connecticut custom, the "Sabbath" commenced at "sundown" on Saturday.

December 24.[1] I set out with the Gentle-womans son who she very civilly offered to go with me when she see no parswasions would cause me to stay which she pressingly desired, and crossing a ferry having but nine miles to New Haven, in a short time arrived there and was Kindly received and well accommodated amongst my Friends and Relations.

The Government of Connecticut Collony begins westward towards York at Stanford[2] (as I am told) and so runs Eastward towards Boston (I mean in my range, because I dont intend to extend my description beyond my own travails) and ends that way at Stonington — And has a great many Large towns lying more northerly. It is a plentiful Country for provisions of all sorts and its Generally Healthy. No one that can and will be dilligent in this place need fear poverty nor the want of food and Rayment.

[1] Madam Knight states that, arriving at Milford, she was entertained till the next night. Probably therefore it was on Monday, the 25th of December, that she went on to New Haven, and the date in the journal is erroneous.

[2] See account of the arbitration in 1650, as to the boundary line.—Palfrey's *New England*, II, 311.

January 6th Being now well Recruited and
fitt for business I discoursed the persons I was
concerned with, that we might finnish in order to
my return to Boston.   They delay[d] as they had
hitherto done hoping to tire my Patience.   But
I was resolute to stay and see an End of the matter let it be never so much to my disadvantage
—So January 9th they come again and promise
the Wednesday following to go through with
the distribution of the Estate which they de-
layed till Thursday and then come with new
amusements.   But at length by the mediation
of that holy good Gentleman, the Rev. Mr.
James Pierpont,[1] the minister of New Haven,
and with the advice and assistance of other our
Good friends we come to an accommodation and
distribution, which having finished though not
till February, the man that waited on me to

[1] Rev. James Pierpont was graduated at Harvard, and in 1685
was ordained at New Haven. He died there in 1714. "In the
pulpit Mr. Pierpont was distinguished among his cotemporaries.
His personal appearance was altogether prepossessing. He was
eminent in the gift of prayer. His doctrine was sound and dis-
criminating and his style was clear, lively and impressive."—
Baron's *Historical Discourses.*

York taking the charge of me I sit out for Boston. We went from New Haven upon the ice (the ferry being not passable thereby) and the Rev. Mr. Pierpont wth Madam Prout[1] Cuzin Trowbridge and divers others were taking leave wee went onward without any thing Remarkabl till wee come to New London and Lodged again at Mr. Saltonstalls—and here I dismist my Guide, and my Generos entertainer provided me Mr. Samuel Rogers[2] of that place to go home with me—I stayed a day here Longer than I intended by the Commands of the Hon[ble] Govenor Winthrop to stay and take a supper with him whose wonderful civility I may not omitt.

[1] John Prout of New Haven, son of Timothy Prout of Boston, married, August 23, 1681, Mary, widow of Daniel Hall and daughter of Henry Rutherford. Sarah, another daughter, was the wife of Thomas Trowbridge, who died in 1702, and who was the father of the Thomas Trowbridge mentioned by Madam Knight. Savage's *Geneal Dictionary.* It is possible therefore that Madam Knight's relationship with the Prout and Trowbridge families was through the Rutherfords.

[2] There were many of this family name at New London. One, possibly a brother of Madam Knight's companion, was the founder of a strange religious sect, of local notoriety; the Rogerenes.

11

The next morning I Crossed ye Ferry to Groton,
having had the Honor of the Company, of Madam Livingston[1] (who is the Govenors Daughter)
and Mary Christophers[2] and divers others to the
boat—And that night Lodg^d at Stonington and
had Rost Beef and pumpkin sause for supper.
The next night at Haven's and had Rost fowle,
and the next day wee come to a river which by
Reason of Y^e Freshetts coming down was swell'd
so high wee fear^d it impassable and the rapid
stream was very terryfying—However we must
over and that in a small Canoo. Mr. Rogers
assuring me of his good Conduct, I after a stay

[1] Mary, the only child of Fitz-John Winthrop, the Governor of
Connecticut, was the wife of Lieut. Col. John Livingston She
died at Uncasville a few miles north of New London, January
8th, 1712-13. She was not buried until the 16th, on account of
the inclemency of the weather and the depth of the snow   A few
months after her death, Col Livingston married Elizabeth, the
only child of Madam Knight, mentioned on a following page

Col. Livingston came from New York to Connecticut after the
failure of the expedition to Canada in 1690, sharing the blame
which was thrown on Gen Winthrop He resided in New London till 1718, and then went to England where he died.

[2] Probably the daughter of Christopher Christophers. The
family of this name was large and influential in New London
and was connected with Madam Knight by marriage

of near an how'r on the shore for consultation
went into the Canoo, and Mr. Rogers paddled
about 100 yards up the Creek by the shore side,
turned into the swift stream and dexterously
steering her in a moment wee come to the other
side as swiftly passing as an arrow shott out of
the Bow by a strong arm. I staid on ye shore
till Hee returned to fetch our horses, which he
caused to swim over himself bringing the furniture in the Cannoo. But it is past my skill to
express the Exceeding fright all their transactions formed in me. Wee were now in the colony of the Massachusetts and taking Lodgings
at the first Inn we come too had a pretty difficult passage the next day which was the second
of March by reason of the sloughy ways then
thawed by the Sunn. Here I mett Capt. John
Richards of Boston who was going home, So
being very glad of his Company we Rode something harder than hitherto, and missing my way
in going up a very steep Hill, my horse dropt
down under me as Dead; this new surprize no
little hurt me meeting it Just at the Entrance

into Dedham from whence we intended to reach
home that night. But was now obliged to gett
another Hors there and leave my own, resolv-
ing for Boston that night if possible. But in
going over the Causeway at Dedham the Bridge
being overflowed by the high waters comming
down I very narrowly escaped falling over into
the river Hors and all wch twas almost a miracle
I did not—now it grew late in the afternoon
and the people having very much discouraged
us about the sloughy way wch they said wee
shoŭld find very difficult and hazardous it so
wrought on mee being tired and dispirited and
disapointed of my desires of going home that I
agreed to Lodg there that night wch wee did at
the house of one Draper, and the next day being
March 3d wee got safe home to Boston, where I
found my aged and tender mother and my Dear
and only Child[1] in good health with open arms
redy to receive me, and my Kind relations and
friends flocking in to welcome mee and hear the

[1] Elizabeth, Madam Knight's only child, then about seventeen,
has already been mentioned in the preface and in a note In the
inventory of her effects, taken after her death, appear the items ,

story of my transactions and travails I having
this day bin five months from home and now I
cannot fully express my Joy and Satisfaction.
But desire sincearly to adore my Great Bene-
factor for thus graciously carying forth and returning in safety his unworthy handmaid.

a negro man and woman; an Indian man, silver plate £234, 13s;
several rings and other jewelry. Acquittances given to the ad-
ministratrix of her estate are signed by the following persons:
Sarah Bass of Boston, widow Mary Bassett of Boston, William
Wyer and Elinor, his wife of Charlestown, Robert Luist, shop-
keeper, of Charlestown, James Fluker and his wife Elizabeth of
Charlestown, Thomas Cheever and his wife Abigail of Chelsea.
Miss Caulkins' *History of New London*, 365, and her letter to W.
R. D.

Note to Providence ferry, page 26

Judge Staples, author of the *Annals of Providence*, is of opinion
that the oldest ferry over the Seekonk river was at Nartow Passage, so called, near where the bridge now is. The riding-over
place across Moshassaek river was at the foot of Steeple Street
See further, *Annals of Providence*, 196, 611. A glance at the map
shows us that Madam Knight does not mention all the rivers or
streams she must have passed through.   E. R. P.

INDEX.

CPSIA information can be obtained
at www.ICGtesting.com
Printed in the USA
BVHW040156080620
581073BV00006B/525

9 781297 778490